THE VENTRILOQUIST

Larry Tremblay

Translated by Keith Turnbull

Talonbooks
Vancouver

Talonbooks
P.O. Box 2076, Vancouver, British Columbia, Canada V6B 3S3
www.talonbooks.com

Typeset in New Baskerville and printed and bound in Canada.

First Printing: 2006

The publisher gratefully acknowledges the financial support of the Canada Council for the Arts; the Government of Canada through the Book Publishing Industry Development Program; and the Province of British Columbia through the British Columbia Arts Council for our publishing activities.

Le Ventriloque was first published in French by Lansman Editeur, Belgium, in 2001. Financial support for this translation provided by the Canada Council for the Arts and the Department of Canadian Heritage through the Book Publishing Industry Development Program.

Library and Archives Canada Cataloguing in Publication

Tremblay, Larry, 1954–
[Ventriloque. English]
The ventriloquist / Larry Tremblay ; translated by Keith Turnbull.

Translation of: Le ventriloque.
A play.
ISBN 0-88922-536-2

I. Turnbull, Keith 1944– II. Title.

PS8589.R445V4513 2006 C842'.54 C2005-906199-5

ISBN-10: 0-88922-536-2
ISBN-13: 978-0-88922-536-7

Le Ventriloque premiered in Paris on March 7, 2001 at the Théâtre International de Langue Française with the following cast and crew:

VENTRILOQUIST/DOCTOR LIMESTONE ...... Hassane Kouyaté
GABY .... Valérie Decobert
LEA .... Magali de Jonckheere

Director .... Gabriel Garran
Set design .... Rodolfo Natale
Special effects .... Abdul Alafrez
Costumes and props .... Valérie Perrier
Sound design .... Pierre-Jean Horville
Lighting design .... Gérard Poll
Assistant director .... Brigitte Villanueva
Artistic coordination .... Emile Herlic

The first Quebec production (by Théâtre PàP) took place in November 2001 at l'Espace Go in Montreal with the following cast and crew:

VENTRILOQUIST/DOCTOR LIMESTONE ...... Frédéric Desager
GABY .... Nathalie Mallette
LENORE/LEA/TALIHUANA .... Nathalie Claude
ALFRED/DOCTOR MORTIMER/BALZAC .... Daniel Parent

Director .... Claude Poissant
Music .... Jean Derome
Set design .... Jean Bard
Costumes .... Marc Sénécal
Lighting design .... Nicolas Descôteaux
Make-up .... Florence Cornet
Movement .... Suzanne Trépanier
Assistant director .... Jean Gaudreau

The English-language premiere of *The Ventriloquist* took place on April 22, 2006 at Factory Theatre in Toronto with the following cast and crew:

VENTRILOQUIST/DOCTOR LIMESTONE . . Nigel Shawn Williams
GABY . . . . Meg Roe
LENORE/LEA/TALIHUANA . . . . Andrea Davis
ALFRED/DOCTOR MORTIMER/BALZAC . . . . Robert Hamilton

Director . . . . Keith Turnbull
Set and costume design . . . . Sue LePage
Lighting design . . . . Michael Kruse
Composition & sound design . . . . Rick Sacks
Dramaturge . . . . Jennifer H. Capraru
Stage manager . . . . Sandy Plunkett
Production manager . . . . Aaron Kelly

Characters

VENTRILOQUIST/DOCTOR LIMESTONE
GABY

LENORE
LEA
ALFRED
DOCTOR MORTIMER
BALZAC
TALIHUANA

A single actor, preferably black, plays the roles of the VENTRILOQUIST and DOCTOR LIMESTONE.

LENORE, LEA and TALIHUANA; ALFRED, DOCTOR MORTIMER and BALZAC are characters of whom we hear only their voices. However, they may be incorporated into the stage action.

Translator's note: The pronunciations of "Mommy" and "Mom" are best determined in consideration of regional diction and character choices.

A Curtain Raiser

A VENTRILOQUIST *manipulates a* DOLL *which looks like a young girl.*

VENTRILOQUIST:
Hello.

DOLL:
Hello.

VENTRILOQUIST:
Have you got something to tell me?

DOLL:
Yesterday was my birthday.

VENTRILOQUIST:
How old were you?

DOLL:
Sixteen.

VENTRILOQUIST:
My, that's good. That's really very good.

DOLL:
It's not all that good.

VENTRILOQUIST:
Sixteen—that's wonderful. That's the best age.

DOLL:
I don't know.

VENTRILOQUIST:
I'm sure you must have had a lovely party for your sixteenth birthday.

DOLL:
No. Yes. No.

VENTRILOQUIST:
Now, something is bothering you. Am I right?

DOLL:
Maybe.

VENTRILOQUIST:
So what happened?

DOLL:
Nothing. I cut off my braids.

VENTRILOQUIST:
I thought I noticed something different.

DOLL:
I took a big pair of scissors and snip! snip!

VENTRILOQUIST:
Your two beautiful braids!

DOLL:
Snip! snip! I watched them disappear into the toilet water whirlpool.

VENTRILOQUIST:
Why did you cut off your braids? And on your sixteenth birthday on top of it all!

DOLL:
I hated them. They made me look ridiculous.

VENTRILOQUIST:
So that's all you have to tell me? Snip! snip! snip! snip! I'm sure your mommy must have given you a beautiful present. What did you ask her for for your birthday?

DOLL:
I asked my mom for a pen for my birthday.

VENTRILOQUIST:
That would never have crossed my mind.

DOLL:
A Parker pen.

VENTRILOQUIST:
A Parker!

DOLL:
A gold-plated Parker!

VENTRILOQUIST:
Nothing but the best!

DOLL:
I love holding heavy shiny things in my hand.

VENTRILOQUIST:
In your little hand! And did your mommy give it to you?

DOLL:
She wanted to scare me.

VENTRILOQUIST:
How?

DOLL:
She wrapped my present up in a big box.

VENTRILOQUIST:
Why?

DOLL:
So I'd think she'd bought me a pair of shoes.

VENTRILOQUIST:
Oh your mommy's nasty.

DOLL:
Yes. No. When I opened the big box, I found another box.

VENTRILOQUIST:
Poor little you! You must have been disappointed?

DOLL:
Yes. My heart froze. I felt sick.

VENTRILOQUIST:
Your little heart had a fright.

DOLL:
Yes. I opened the second box and I found another box.

VENTRILOQUIST:
Not another one!

DOLL:
I saw red. I had smoke coming out my ears.

VENTRILOQUIST:
I'm glad I wasn't there.

DOLL:
I opened the third box; I found another box.

VENTRILOQUIST:
What a nightmare!

DOLL:
I started to cry. I had trouble breathing. I opened the fourth box. I found another box.

VENTRILOQUIST:
That's terrible!

DOLL:
I started to bleed.

VENTRILOQUIST:
To bleed! What you just said is very interesting. To bleed! But why? What happened?

DOLL:
Nothing. I lost blood, that's all. I opened the fifth box.

VENTRILOQUIST:
I hope you finally found what you wanted.

DOLL:
No way! There was still another box.

VENTRILOQUIST:
Oh my my my, it just gets worse and worse!

DOLL:
I ended up with my mouth full.

VENTRILOQUIST:
What do you mean?

DOLL:
Full of saliva!

VENTRILOQUIST:
Full of saliva!?

DOLL:
Green, yellow, blue saliva.

VENTRILOQUIST:
It's extraordinary all this happened to you!

DOLL:
Yes. No. It's disgusting. I spit, spit, spit on the people.

VENTRILOQUIST:
Which people?

DOLL:
My parents, my friends.

VENTRILOQUIST:
You spit on them?

DOLL:
Yes. That calmed me down. I opened the sixth box. My mother was laughing like a madwoman. Well she would wouldn't she — I found another box. I wanted to bite her.

VENTRILOQUIST:
Your mother!

DOLL:
Yes. And everyone else!

VENTRILOQUIST:
One must learn a little self-control in life.

DOLL:
They were making fun of me. They were singing stupid songs.

VENTRILOQUIST:
What songs?

DOLL:
Love songs but there was nothing but derision in their voices. I hurried and opened the seventh, then the eighth, then the ninth, I wanted to shoot them all, all of them, ratatatatat!

VENTRILOQUIST:
Stop, stop, you're getting nasty! You're going over the top. It was only a game. I am sure no one wanted to hurt you!

DOLL:
You too, another doink! A stupid adult doink!

VENTRILOQUIST:
What did you just say?

DOLL:
You heard me.

VENTRILOQUIST:
And why am I a stupid adult doink?

DOLL:
'Cause you're just like the rest of them. Because you're like everyone else. You don't understand me.

VENTRILOQUIST:
And you?

DOLL:
What about me?

VENTRILOQUIST:
You're not like everyone else?

DOLL:
I'm different.

Silence. Unease.

VENTRILOQUIST:
Are you sulking?

DOLL:
You're the one that's sulking.

VENTRILOQUIST:
Not at all at all. Sulking, no, that's not my style.

DOLL:
Me neither.

VENTRILOQUIST:
So.

DOLL:
So what?

VENTRILOQUIST:
Are you going to finish your story?

DOLL:
You're not interested.

VENTRILOQUIST:
Yes I am. Continue, go on.

DOLL:
I don't want to anymore.

VENTRILOQUIST:
See, you are sulking.

DOLL:
I'm not sulking.

VENTRILOQUIST:
Then finish your story.

DOLL:
You really want to hear the rest?

VENTRILOQUIST:
Absolutely.

DOLL:
OK. When I opened the ninth box, I found/

VENTRILOQUIST:
/another box.

DOLL:
Yes, the tenth. I had to open it with the tips of my fingernails.

VENTRILOQUIST:
Why?

DOLL:
Think about it! It was so small I was afraid of crushing it with my fingers.

VENTRILOQUIST:
Ah!

DOLL:
And again I found another box — this time, tiny, tiny, tiny! Everybody held their breath.

VENTRILOQUIST:
And how did you open it this time?

DOLL:
I opened it with a hair.

VENTRILOQUIST:
What! I don't believe you!

DOLL:
Yes, yes, with a hair! It took forever. I almost died!

VENTRILOQUIST:
And then?

DOLL:
Everyone went "ahhh"!

VENTRILOQUIST:
Why?

DOLL:
Because there was nothing more to see!

VENTRILOQUIST:
Nothing more?

DOLL:
Nothing more. I went up to my bedroom and I came back with something in my hands.

VENTRILOQUIST:
What?

DOLL:
Guess!

VENTRILOQUIST:
I don't like guessing.

DOLL:
A magnifying glass!

VENTRILOQUIST:
You have your own magnifying glass?

DOLL:
To look at my stamp collection.

VENTRILOQUIST:
And did you see anything with your magnifying glass?

DOLL:
A box!

VENTRILOQUIST:
The twelfth!

DOLL:
Yes, the twelfth! And you know what? It opened by itself! All by itself! All I had to do was look at it and it opened!

VENTRILOQUIST:
Unbelievable! And what did you see when the twelfth box opened by itself? Not another box, I hope?

DOLL:
No.

VENTRILOQUIST:
No?

DOLL:
No. I saw … I saw …

VENTRILOQUIST:
… yes, you saw, you saw …

DOLL:
I saw … I saw … a hole!

VENTRILOQUIST:
You're making this up.

DOLL:
I swear! I saw a key-shaped hole! The smallest key-hole in the whole world, in the whole universe even! I leaned over it with my magnifying glass. I looked in the hole and I saw … I saw … I saw …

The curtain opens. A room more empty than full. Gaby *writes.*

Gaby:

Once upon a time there was a young girl …

She thinks, then crosses it out.

… Once upon a time there was a young man … a young man of great beauty. He was called … Martin … no … Anthony … no … Andrew … no … Charles …

A fly buzzes and disturbs Gaby. *She tries to shoo it away without success. Finally she spears it with her pen and goes back to her story.*

Once upon a time there was a young man of great beauty. He bore the evocative name of … of …

She looks at the fly she just killed.

… of Flyback! Since his eyes contained the shimmering reflections of a fly speared by the sun. This young man carried himself like a … like a young man. What he didn't know was that he was in reality a … a … a—n onion! "Pooh! A vulgar onion!" One day, a young girl sees Flyback, falls in love at first sight, courts him and finally obtains what she covets — a deep kiss.

Knocking is heard at the door.

Lenore:

Gaby! Gaby! You've locked your door again! I really wonder what you do in there.

Gaby:

You know!

LENORE:

Spending all your time locked up in your room is not normal for a girl your age — on your birthday, on top of it all!

GABY:

Can a girl my age be normal?

LENORE:

Your friend Lea is downstairs. She's waiting for you in the living room.

GABY:

She's not my friend anymore.

LENORE:

She brought you a present.

GABY:

I don't want any presents.

LENORE:

You are being really disagreeable, Gaby. You could at least make an effort on your birthday.

GABY:

Why do I have to make all the effort?

LENORE:

You get on my nerves when you talk back to me like that! Come down right away, it's not polite to keep Lea waiting.

GABY:

I'm coming! Tell her to wait two minutes. I'm just finishing a sentence.

LENORE:

Oh you and your sentences!

GABY goes back to work writing.

GABY:

One day, a young girl sees Flyback, falls in love at first sight, courts him and finally obtains what she covets — a deep kiss. Then the girl discovers that she has courted an onion. She runs away and goes to rinse her mouth out in the frigid waters of a spring. Flyback will never unlock his lips again. He … he falls sick … no … he decides to … no, no, that's not it … Flyback will never unlock his lips again and he lets himself die of hunger. That's it! And after? After … after, a peasant finds … no … discovers the body at the root of a tree stump, he buries it in the garden. That year is particularly cold. Snow covers all the fields. In the spring, the peasant is surprised to see his garden more beautiful than ever. Well before harvest time, he takes in his potatoes, his cabbages and his onions and joyously brings them to his wife to prepare a fine soup. When the peasant's wife slices the onions, a smell of … of … roses escapes from them. Tears of joy moisten her eyes. The more she slices the onions, the more she laughs and laughs and laughs from happiness! Since that day, instead of the reek of boiled cabbage, the peasant's house exudes a rose perfume!

Singing and dancing, GABY euphorically repeats the last sentence. We again hear knocks at the door.

LENORE:

Gaby, this is the last time I'm telling you: come down right now!

GABY:

I'm coming! I'm coming!

LENORE:

Would you mind telling me just what you're up to in there?

GABY:

You know very well.

LENORE:

No, I don't know. Why are you shutting yourself up in your room?

GABY:

I'm coming; I'm getting dressed!

LENORE:

Open the door!

GABY:

I'll open it when I'm ready. I'm old enough to decide what I want to do.

LENORE:

If you don't open this door right away, you will not get your birthday present; I'm going to throw it in the garbage. (*Beat.*) D'you hear me? (*Beat.*) I'm serious. (*Beat.*) I'm going to do it, Gaby. You know I will.

GABY opens the door. Time and space teeter-totter. DOCTOR LIMESTONE comes into the room but one has the impression instead that GABY arrives.

GABY:

Doctor Limestone?

DOCTOR LIMESTONE:

The same.

GABY:

I am Gaby Wrenfield. I have an appointment with you.

DOCTOR LIMESTONE:

You are early.

GABY:

I am early? (*looks at her watch*) But it is three o'clock by my watch. I am sure I made an appointment for three o'clock, did I not?

DOCTOR LIMESTONE:

Exactly. But by my watch, it is two thirty-three and a bit.

GABY:

Perhaps your watch has stopped.

DOCTOR LIMESTONE:

My watch has never done that on me. It is a quality watch. I paid a good deal for it. I always insist on watches of the very highest quality. And I always pay a good deal for them. It is a Mortimer. It is the third Mortimer I have purchased. I lost the first. They stole the second. I look after the third, this one, like the apple of my eye. It is therefore out of the question that my watch, a Mortimer, might lose nearly thirty minutes. No, no, you are early.

GABY:

But this watch is practically new.

DOCTOR LIMESTONE:

You know, there are people who manipulate time with their watches—be they of high or of mediocre quality—in order to align true with false, the good with the bad. This is certainly not true in your case. But come in! I was going to have a coffee. I always have a coffee between my two afternoon sessions. But since you are here, I shall have my coffee later.

GABY:

That's very kind of you, Doctor Limestone.

DOCTOR LIMESTONE:

Are you aware of my method?

GABY:

By all means. I have watched your informational program on television many times.

DOCTOR LIMESTONE:

Read this.

He takes a prospectus from his pocket.

GABY:

What is it?

DOCTOR LIMESTONE:

Read it. You will see.

GABY:

But I have watched your program many times, Doctor Lime …

DOCTOR LIMESTONE:

Read.

GABY reads.

It is my new prospectus. I never could get used to the old one. The layout did not show off the contents to advantage. This one is much more effective: a paper fitting to the touch, a much clearer typeface. The text floats upon a pastel background. It is so much better. It reads well, does it not?

GABY:

Yes, Doctor Limestone, it reads very well.

DOCTOR LIMESTONE:

Well unfold it! I expose the essentials inside!

GABY:

(*reading*) "Doctor Limestone's Therapeutic Method."

DOCTOR LIMESTONE:

Read it, read it.

As soon as GABY *begins to read the prospectus, he snatches it out of her hands.*

Is it clear ?

GABY:
I think … I think so, Doctor Limestone.

DOCTOR LIMESTONE:
Do we agree?

GABY:
We … agree, Doctor Limestone.

DOCTOR LIMESTONE:
Then if we agree and we do, do we not, we can proceed.

GABY *wants to sit down.*

No, do not sit down quite yet. Tell me first what brings you here to me.

GABY:
I suffer from a serious block. I am a writer.

DOCTOR LIMESTONE:
You are a writer! Very good, excellent even!

GABY:
Yes, Doctor Limestone, I am a writer but I am incapable of writing a single line.

DOCTOR LIMESTONE:
And you suffered this block right from the very beginning?

GABY:
No, no, Doctor Limestone. Just for the last four years.

DOCTOR LIMESTONE:
That is very good.

GABY:

Four years ago my brother died. Perhaps you have already heard of him: Edgar Wrenfield?

DOCTOR LIMESTONE:

Actually no.

GABY:

He was also a writer. He published *Midnight Deluge.*

DOCTOR LIMESTONE:

Very good.

GABY:

A book of poetry.

DOCTOR LIMESTONE:

Very very good.

GABY:

His book won the Eldred-Woodworth Prize. A prize awarded to recognize promising talent.

DOCTOR LIMESTONE:

Never, in all my life, have I read a book of poetry.

GABY:

It is a magnificent book. I know it by heart.

DOCTOR LIMESTONE:

Very good. Your brother, then, died four years ago.

GABY:

Yes, Doctor Limestone, my brother died. The autopsy carried out on his body revealed that Edgar had suffered atrocious pain before dying. The forensic doctors found traces of an extremely rare poison in his stomach. They also found a four-centimetre long needle driven into the roof of his mouth. They had noticed, previously, that his wrists had been cut, that his thighs, his feet, his sex had been burned. X-rays also revealed fractures in his legs and his toes. But above all, above all, Edgar's tongue had disappeared. According to the experts, it had been neither cut nor torn out, but not one of them could explain how it had been separated from its root. Not one.

Doctor Limestone:
Very good. Very very good. Really very good.

Gaby:
Doctor Limestone?

Doctor Limestone:
Yes.

Gaby:
Help me find my muse again.

Doctor Limestone:
Sit down.

Gaby:
Help me, Doctor Limestone.

Doctor Limestone:
Sit down, Gaby.

Gaby:
Yes, Doctor Limestone.

Doctor Limestone:
Relax. Breathe calmly. Relax. (*after a moment*) Are you fully relaxed?

Gaby:
Very relaxed, Doctor Limestone.

Doctor Limestone:
Then I will proceed. I am going to count to three. You see, it is very simple. One … two … three. How do you feel?

Gaby:
Very well.

DOCTOR LIMESTONE:
Tell me what you are thinking at the moment.

GABY:
...

DOCTOR LIMESTONE:
Do you not wish to answer this question?

GABY:
No, Doctor. I mean: yes, yes, certainly, I want to answer this question but I don't know what I think. I mean: I don't know what I think exactly. I think, yes, we think, we, I mean, I but also you and all people, yes we think all the time and sometimes we don't think that we are in the midst of thinking and if you ask me what I think at the moment, I don't know if I/

DOCTOR LIMESTONE:
Take off your gloves and your hat.

GABY:
What?

DOCTOR LIMESTONE:
The prospectus.

GABY:
What?

GABY wears neither gloves nor hat.

DOCTOR LIMESTONE:
You read it carefully?

GABY:
Yes, Doctor Limestone.

DOCTOR LIMESTONE:
Take off your gloves and your hat.

GABY:
But ...

DOCTOR LIMESTONE:
The prospectus.

GABY:
The prospectus?

DOCTOR LIMESTONE:
"Doctor Limestone's Therapeutic Method." Do we fully agree?

GABY:
Yes, Doctor Limestone.

DOCTOR LIMESTONE:
You will see, it gives astonishing results. Astonishing, Gaby. Proceed.

GABY:
But, Doctor Limestone, I'm not/

DOCTOR LIMESTONE:
(*firmly*) Proceed!

GABY:
I'm proceeding, Doctor Limestone, I'm proceeding.

GABY mimes taking off gloves and a hat.

DOCTOR LIMESTONE:
Very good. Very very good. Excellent even. Sit back down. Open your heart.

GABY:
I am sitting back down. I am opening my heart. (*Beat.*) How Doctor Limestone? How do I open my heart?

DOCTOR LIMESTONE:
Speak, Gaby. It is also in the prospectus: you must speak.

GABY:
I am speaking, Doctor Limestone.

GABY tries to speak but nothing comes out.

DOCTOR LIMESTONE:

Let yourself go, Gaby. You see, it is very simple. I count up to three. After three, you speak.

GABY:

Very simple, Doctor Limestone. After three, I speak.

DOCTOR LIMESTONE:

One, two, three.

GABY:

(*all in one breath*) I wear braids. I am convinced that wearing braids—one to the right, one to the left, the two exactly the same length—is the only way not to lose my head. I take maniacal care braiding my hair. I can redo this operation many times a day with patience and dexterity. I have a lot of both. I am proud of myself and I detest everyone around me without knowing why.

DOCTOR LIMESTONE:

A very good start. Really a very good start. Go on, Gaby.

GABY:

One morning, I lock myself in the bathroom with a pair of scissors. I am careful to push the latch on the door so that neither my father nor my mother come and interrupt what I have decided to undertake. It is a Saturday. The very day of my sixteenth birthday. I cut my two braids and throw them in the toilet. Then I open the door, I go into the living room where the telephone is. I call my best friend Lea. Her mother answers and tells me Lea is still sleeping. I scream at her "Wake her up!" When Lea starts chattering on the other end of the line, I interrupt her by pouring abominable abuse into the receiver. Never in all my life had I uttered so many vulgar, shameful, odious words. Spewing them forth, I experience an enormous relief. I don't know why I behave like this. Lea is my only friend. Before hanging up the phone, I make her swear not to come to my birthday party. She replies that I am mad and that madwomen don't deserve to have birthday parties.

Doctor Limestone:
Do you feel like crying?

Gaby:
No, Doctor Limestone.

Doctor Limestone:
Are you certain?

Gaby:
Absolutely certain, Doctor Limestone.

He mumbles something incomprehensible.

Pardon me?

Doctor Limestone:
Gaby, you are too healthy to understand what is happening to you. You ought to experience a profound deterioration. Be aware that you are ridiculous to look at — extremely repugnant to look at. Are you aware of that?

Gaby:
I don't know. Yes maybe so. So much escapes us after all.

Doctor Limestone:
Don't talk just for the sake of talking.

Gaby:
But it is very difficult to answer your/

Doctor Limestone:
Do not hide your body with your arms. Let yourself go. Relax. I feel you are nervous. (*with the firmness of a command*) Cry, for goodness' sake cry!

GABY:

Yes, Doctor Limestone, I am crying.

GABY cries. Knocking is heard at the door.

LENORE:

Gaby, what's wrong?

GABY:

Nothing, Mommy.

LENORE:

I'm not crazy. There's something going on in there.

GABY:

No there's not.

LENORE:

You're not like other girls your age.

GABY:

Mom, don't start.

LENORE:

Well. Very well. You don't want to talk you don't want to talk, it's up to you, but don't come crying to me when it's too late.

GABY:

Too late?

LENORE:

Yes, Gaby: when it's too late.

GABY:

What are you talking about?

LENORE:

Don't play innocent with me.

GABY:

You're getting on my nerves!

LENORE:

Don't forget you have an appointment shortly with Doctor Mortimer.

GABY:

Yes, yes!

LENORE:

Put on clean underwear.

GABY:

Oh, Mom!

LENORE:

I have to tell you. You're so absent-minded.

GABY:

I am not absent-minded; I'm just preoccupied.

LENORE:

Now hurry up down, Doctor Mortimer does not tolerate lateness. Then after that, we'll go to the hair salon. It's your birthday, I want you to be pretty.

GABY:

Yes Mommy.

DOCTOR LIMESTONE:

Good. How do you feel?

GABY:

Sad, weak, lost.

DOCTOR LIMESTONE:

Excellent. You are making truly remarkable progress. Go on.

GABY:

Pardon me?

DOCTOR LIMESTONE:

Go on. Speak! You must speak!

GABY:
Yes, Doctor Limestone.

DOCTOR LIMESTONE:
I am counting to three.

GABY:
That isn't necessary.

DOCTOR LIMESTONE:
I insist. It is in the prospectus.

GABY:
If it is in the prospectus.

DOCTOR LIMESTONE:
I am counting: one, two, three. Go on, Gaby.

GABY:
Yes, Doctor Limestone. I'm going on. The day of my sixteenth birthday, when my mother notices my hair is cut, she throws the cake she's made into the garbage. She sends me to my room. I vowed a ferocious hatred for my mother. Then, seized by remorse, I am swamped with shame. Some weeks before, I had asked my mother to give me, for my sixteenth birthday, a Parker pen, a gold-plated Parker. When I say that I had "asked," I mean I had used every possible angle to convince my mother to get me exactly this birthday present. I had been firm, saccharine, outrageous, obsequious, intense, threatening, scheming, overflowing with love — ingenious. Towards the end of the afternoon, my mother finally opens the door to my room. Her eyes are red but she holds, in her hands, a package of joy. She hands me it without saying a word. I open the package. I rejoice. I — Gaby, sixteen years old — am going to be a great writer. I feel the weight of the pen. It is heavy and shiny. I'm burning to inscribe in my lined notebooks with my favourite ink — the colour of the Caribbean

Sea — the words which constitute my masterpiece. I open a notebook, I write. The words escape without the slightest effort from the aqua nib of the Parker. I am carried along on a gentle, regular flow that gives my sentences a classical breadth. The story which fills my little notebook, page after page, concerns my friend Lea. Lea, the day of her best friend's sixteenth birthday, decides to give the most beautiful present her modest means allow—her collection of stamps, her most precious possession. The story is nothing but pages and pages describing the beauty of Lea's favourite stamps, stamps from Africa in the vibrant colours of wild animals sparkling with a sumptuous vocabulary. When I close my notebook, I cry tears of joy. In bed, I turn over and over in my mind all the stories I am going to write. I can't wait to get up, to take my Parker and to open another notebook. In the morning, my mother wakes me. She informs me that my friend Lea is waiting for me in the living room. I hurry downstairs to meet her, surprised to see her turn up after all the insults I had showered over her on the phone. She was sitting, all coifed, all turned out in a dress made out of a childish print; beside her is a large package which she quickly gives me. Embarrassed, I give her a hug and then open the package. Her stamp collection! Exactly as I had written! I faint. That evening, in my room, I try to think it through: "Gaby, why did you insult Lea on the phone?" I answer: "Because she deserves it. Because I don't want to be like those stupid little girls who think that the world doesn't revolve around them. Because I am not like them. Because I am different. Because I — I have a destiny. Because. Because." Because I am not insane. Before I fainted that very morning in the living room I had already foreseen everything! In the most unsuspected corner of my heart, an eye had opened. It could see — sparkling within the thickest shadows of monotony — the unique and the fabulous.

DOCTOR LIMESTONE:
And what had you foreseen?

GABY:
The unimaginable. That very night, I inscribed to paper a second story. When I lay the gold-plated Parker back down, I could finally fall asleep, now relaxed, having written throughout most of the night breathlessly pursuing my inspiration. But I am delighted. I have given birth to a small masterpiece. Enclosed within my notebook, well sealed by the barbed wire of my sentences, is a story about a woman who chances upon her daughter — the day of her sixteenth birthday — in the midst of cutting off her two magnificent braids. She snatches the pair of scissors from her hands, lifts her arm, and then —

DOCTOR LIMESTONE:
And then?

GABY:
And then she—she too—cuts her hair! That is the story I had written!

DOCTOR LIMESTONE:
Excellent, excellent. Go on.

GABY:
In the morning, in bed, I stand on the bridge of a ship tossed onto the open seas without hope of return. In my veins flows the snake of genius which makes my wrists swell and ache. No longer do I take part in day by day routine but rather I experience the dazzle of adventure.

DOCTOR LIMESTONE:
And why, Gaby?

GABY:
Because ... because that very morning, when my mother opens the door of my room, the vision she

presents confirms my late night intuition. My mother, my tender and ferocious mother appears in the frame of the door, her head shaved. There are traces of dried blood on her skull.

DOCTOR LIMESTONE:
Excellent, excellent.

GABY:
I am now certain of it: everything I write with the gold-plated Parker comes to pass one way or another.

Knocking is heard at the door.

LEA:
Gaby? Gaby? It's Lea. Your mother gave me permission to come up. May I see you?

GABY:
Get lost!

LEA:
I don't hold it against you. You know — what you said to me yesterday on the telephone — I don't hold it against you. Quite the opposite, I'm grateful. It's very good to have a friend like you.

GABY:
You got it.

LEA:
What are you doing?

GABY:
You know.

LEA:
All those things that you said to me, you know, I can't stop thinking about them.

GABY:
I apologize. I shouldn't have. I wasn't thinking. I don't know what came over me.

LEA:

No, no. Don't apologize. I talked to God about it. Well — you know what I mean. I talk to God every night before going to sleep. He explained everything to me. Don't worry. I'm here. I want to help you. You wounded me deeply yesterday. You said nasty things to me. No one but you has ever humiliated me like that. Where did you learn such vulgar, shameful, icky things?

GABY:

What are you talking about? I just called you jerk-off, cum-sucker, shit ass, dolly slit, little cunt, fat cunt, dirty bitch, church harlot, black asshole/

LEA:

Stop! Stop! You're only hurting yourself/

GABY:

... red asshole, infected hag, little pig girl, pink slut, yellow slut/

LEA:

Stop!

GABY:

green slut, pack of wet rags/

LEA:

Stop, Gaby, you're destroying yourself! Your mother asked me to help you. Open the door. God ordered me to save you. We love you, Gaby, God and I, we love you!

GABY:

Die!

DOCTOR LIMESTONE:

How do you feel?

GABY:

Nasty, perverse, disgusting.

DOCTOR LIMESTONE:
Excellent, excellent. Take off your coat.

GABY isn't wearing one.

Gaby:
But, Doctor Limestone, I am not wearing a/

DOCTOR LIMESTONE:
Take off your coat! The prospectus, Gaby, the prospectus! It is in the prospectus! Take off your coat!

GABY:
Very good, very very good.

She mimes taking off a coat.

DOCTOR LIMESTONE:
What progress, what progress! Go on.

GABY:
Balzac.

DOCTOR LIMESTONE:
Pardon me?

GABY:
I'm going on, Doctor Limestone, I'm going on: Balzac.

DOCTOR LIMESTONE:
Very good, even very very good, Balzac, certainly, go on, go on.

GABY:
Balzac. Thanks to the gold-plated Parker, I am going to catch up to the idol of my adolescence: Balzac! Even better: I am going to overtake him. Do you understand?

DOCTOR LIMESTONE:
Certainly. But how, Gaby, how are you going to overtake Balzac?

GABY:

Very simply. Can't you guess? All I have to do is write another story. Once upon a time there was a young girl. The day of her sixteenth birthday/

DOCTOR LIMESTONE:

Yes, yes, I'm beginning to know it/

GABY:

she severs the two braids that she wore/

DOCTOR LIMESTONE:

in a ridiculous symmetrical fashion/

GABY:

As soon as she observes them disappear …

DOCTOR LIMESTONE:

into the toilet water whirlpool/

GABY:

she feels a powerful transformation beginning. She can no longer permit herself to play at just being a little girl wrapped in floral prints. She opens a notebook and writes, without ever rubbing or crossing out/

DOCTOR LIMESTONE:

the most beautiful novel in the world.

GABY:

Yes, Doctor Limestone, the most beautiful novel in the world! As soon as I finish writing this story, a growling — as if a dog were sitting inside my chest — makes me shake from head to toe. The transformation takes over. Again I take hold of the Parker and, just like I had just written … I begin to write the most beautiful novel in the world.

Knocking is heard at the door.

LENORE:

Gaby, guess what I have in my hand?

GABY:

My birthday present?

LENORE:

No. A postcard.

GABY:

From Edgar?

LENORE:

Aha!

GABY:

It's from him, isn't it, I'm right, it's from him? What's he say? Is he well?

LENORE:

Guess where he is.

GABY:

Africa.

LENORE:

How do you know?

GABY:

I … I guessed. You asked me to guess, I guessed. Is he well? Is Edgar well? (*Beat.*) Mom, you're there? (*Beat.*) I know you're there. Answer me. Tell me if Edgar is well. What did he write on the postcard?

LENORE:

He wishes you a happy birthday.

GABY:

That's all?

LENORE:

Gaby, tell me the truth now, has something already happened between you and your brother?

GABY:

What do you mean?

LENORE:

Nothing. I don't mean anything. As usual, Gaby, I don't mean anything.

DOCTOR LIMESTONE:

Take off your shoes. Take off your shoes. Take off your shoes, Gaby!

GABY:

It's in the prospectus?

DOCTOR LIMESTONE:

Yes, yes, certainly.

She imitates taking them off even though she is wearing shoes.

No! No! No! You must take them off for real! You must take another step. You need certainties. I am offering you the chance to get out of your deep depression. Because you are deeply depressive, are you not? Keep up with me. Take off your shoes, and so, experience the relief. You deserve it. Release yourself!

She hesitates, pulls herself together, then takes off her shoes.

Do not forget that everything depends on your capacity to descend into total ignominy. You are just trash, debris. Appreciate our relationship. Without me, you suffer. Admit it. Say it!

GABY:

What, Doctor Limestone?

DOCTOR LIMESTONE:

Say clearly: Without Doctor Limestone, I suffer.

GABY:

Without Doctor Limestone, I suffer.

DOCTOR LIMESTONE:

Have you found relief by taking off your shoes?

GABY:

Yes, at last yes, yes it is undeniable, I think so, no I don't think so, it's more than that, yes I felt a—yes that's it, that's exactly it—a relief, Doctor Limestone.

DOCTOR LIMESTONE:

Listen, Gaby, do not play with my nerves. We are at a crucial stage in our therapeutic relationship. When I ask if by taking off your shoes you find relief, answer: yes, Doctor Limestone. Is that clear?

GABY:

But that is what I said, Doctor ...

DOCTOR LIMESTONE:

Go on.

GABY:

Yes, Doctor Limestone. I am going on. I take four months to write the most beautiful novel in the world. As soon as I come home from school, I lock myself in my room, plunge the nib of my Parker into the ink well and pump the ink imagining the surge of turquoise waves on the lined pages of my notebooks. The precise moment when I feel the ink rise into the reservoir fills me with a gnashing power. Then my veins inflate and I seem to hear them howling.

DOCTOR LIMESTONE:

Ah! Ah!

GABY:

What, Doctor Limestone?

DOCTOR LIMESTONE:

Pay no attention to me. Go ahead, gallop on.

GABY:

I am going ahead, Doctor Limestone. I am galloping on. (*very fast*) Since beginning to write the most beautiful novel in the world, cleanliness becomes secondary. I hardly eat. I no longer go to church on Sundays and, on top of all that, I no longer have any interest in my classmates whom I consider inferior. Even my professors seem like midgets or marionettes. What do they know of the real world? How can they pretend to communicate a vision of the world? From their mouths escape nothing but clichés and pregurgitated ideas. I pity them. They have no idea who is really sitting silently in front of them, impatient to leave their world of banalities and platitudes to regain the vertigo of creation. As soon as I set foot back in my room, gusts of genius tremble through the walls. I take off the ridiculous clothes school rules force me to wear and I disappear into a thick dressing gown. Then, I open my notebooks. My back bent, my head tilted, my right hand drawn to the Parker which runs after the words escaping from its golden nib, I plunge. Never has a writer written as I have done! After a week, exalted by dozens and dozens of scribbled pages, by the unbridled characters that spring out of my imagination, I decide to sleep no more. A writer of my calibre goes without sleep. Why lose precious hours in bed when the most beautiful novel in the world is still unfinished? To keep my edge, I drink coffee. I drink an ocean of coffee. Among the innumerable substances which have stayed in or passed through the organs of my body, it is coffee which tops the list for quantity. I am convinced of it. Coffee.

DOCTOR LIMESTONE:

Coffee. Very good. Very very very good.

He mumbles something.

GABY:
What are you saying?

He mumbles again.

I do not understand, Doctor Limestone.

He mumbles again.

I don't understand!

DOCTOR LIMESTONE:
Take off your dress.

GABY:
What?

DOCTOR LIMESTONE:
Take off your dress! And don't try that mime trick on me again. Enough of that!

GABY:
You are losing your mind, Doctor Limestone!

DOCTOR LIMESTONE:
The prospectus! Take off your dress!

GABY:
But I do not see why I/

DOCTOR LIMESTONE:
So why did you take off your shoes? Why?

GABY:
Because you asked me to, that's all!

DOCTOR LIMESTONE:
Then take off your dress when I ask you to!

GABY:
But there is a difference between shoes and/

DOCTOR LIMESTONE:
Gaby, I'm counting to three. At three proceed.

GABY:
What is happening to you?

DOCTOR LIMESTONE:
One, two, three.

A beat. They stare intensely at each other.

GABY:
If it's written in the/

DOCTOR LIMESTONE:
It is written.

As GABY takes off her dress, knocking is heard at the door.

ALFRED:
Gaby, it's your father. I have two things to say to you.

GABY:
I'm busy.

ALFRED:
Lea told me everything. Go and apologize to her.

GABY:
Lea's insane. She's a liar.

ALFRED:
Right now your mother is crying in the kitchen. She worked all day for you. If you'd only seen the cake she made for you. I don't understand you, Gaby. Why are you so nasty? Everyone loves you and all you do is say monstrous things to your best friend. Why did you do that?

GABY:
I didn't do anything wrong.

ALFRED:
And now, what are you up to behind this door, eh?

GABY:

Nothing. Nothing. I'm doing nothing.

ALFRED:

Neither your mother nor I taught you to talk like a tart. It's all those books you read secretly in your room. That's enough of that, do you hear me Gaby? Enough of that. I'm going to throw them all in the fire. Open this door! Do you hear me, open it!

DOCTOR LIMESTONE:

How do you feel?

GABY:

I don't know.

DOCTOR LIMESTONE:

The success of my method depends on the strength of conviction that possesses the underwear. That surprises you doesn't it?

GABY shakes her head yes. He exhales loudly.

Stand up straight. Everything's caving in on you, but don't show it. Stand up straight because everything is caving in on you like the floors of a house which fall one on top of each other from the attic to the cellar. How do you feel?

GABY:

I don't know. I don't know anymore.

DOCTOR LIMESTONE:

Don't run away from it. Answer my question: How do you feel?

GABY:

I have a stomach ache. I want to vomit. I wish I could fall through the floor.

DOCTOR LIMESTONE:

Aha! Excellent!

He moves closer to her.

You have goose bumps. What is underwear? That is the question. I have a story to tell you too. One day, my mother punished me. You know why? I had stolen money from her pig to buy me candies. My mother had an enormous pig. You know what I mean: a bank shaped like a pig — a piggy bank. I managed to extricate some change from her big pig to buy myself some candy. My mother, a very suspicious person, had noticed it. She tied me to a chair, in my underwear, and made me drink onion soup. I abhor onion soup. I abhor all shapes and forms of onions: in photos, in soups certainly, in salads, in quiches. Onions repulse me. The day when my mother made me swallow — tied to a chair — an entire bowl of onion soup, I understood the strength of conviction of underwear. What is underwear? Answer me! What is underwear?

GABY:

I don't know Doctor Limestone. But in fact, yes, of course, I know what underwear is, it is precisely what I am wearing at this very moment but you ask the question in such a way that it is very difficult to answer your/

DOCTOR LIMESTONE:

Shut up.

He touches her with the tips of his fingers.

Always goose bumps. Why? Are you cold?

GABY:

Yes, Doctor Limestone.

DOCTOR LIMESTONE:

It's very hot in here. Really very hot. I — I'm very very hot. It's unacceptable, Gaby. I can't bear this contradiction. Not at all at all!

GABY:
I don't understand, Doctor Limestone.

DOCTOR LIMESTONE:
Call me Bob.

GABY:
Bob?

DOCTOR LIMESTONE:
Bob. Realize the nothingness you inspire. Sink, Gaby sink down step by step into profound sensations of loss.

GABY:
I'm sinking, Doctor Limestone, I'm sinking.

DOCTOR LIMESTONE:
Bob. Call me Bob.

GABY:
Yes, Bob.

DOCTOR LIMESTONE:
D'you like standing in front of Bob in your underwear—you delicate little piece of trash?

Knocking is heard at the door.

DOCTOR MORTIMER:
Gaby, it's Doctor Mortimer here. Your mother asked me to come by to see you. I hope you are taking into consideration the exceptional nature of this situation. I never, but never, go to my patients' homes. It is only because your mother insisted. Poor woman! She even got down on her knees in front of me. Had I not raised her up, she was going to kiss my shoes. Now, it seems you have some problems?

GABY:
I don't have any problems, Doctor Mortimer.

DOCTOR MORTIMER:
Open the door, Gaby. I have to examine you.

GABY:
I'm busy, Doctor Mortimer.

DOCTOR MORTIMER:
It won't take long. Remember our last appointment. It will be just the same.

GABY:
Just the same, Doctor Mortimer?

DOCTOR MORTIMER:
Exactly: just the same. It didn't hurt last time. It will be just the same this time. Open, Gaby, open up.

DOCTOR LIMESTONE:
How do you feel? Are you still cold?

GABY:
No, no, not at all, not at all at all, Bob. I'm very hot.

DOCTOR LIMESTONE:
Excellent. What progress, what progress! Go on.

GABY:
I'm going on, Bob. I spend sleepless nights drinking black coffee, liquefied in my polluted dressing gown. I write, I write and I get older. Every two or three days my stack of notebooks grows. My fingers, blue with ink, stain my face, my thighs. My characters burn in my belly. Meteors fly out of my guts. Lightning flashes from my bones. If—yes, if someone had got into my room and tore me away from my desk, had interrupted me at my work, were it only for a second, I would leap at their face and rip their two eyes out with my teeth. But no one came to interrupt the writing of the most beautiful novel in the world. After four months, the words *THE END* came like a spasm out of the nib of my Parker. I had beaten Balzac.

DOCTOR LIMESTONE:
That's very good. That's even very good.

GABY:
Yes, Bob, it's very good but how to be convinced? How to be certain that the twelve notebooks piled on the corner of my table, near my bed, make up the most beautiful novel in the world? Only one person could assure me.

DOCTOR LIMESTONE:
Your brother.

GABY:
Yes, Bob. I put my twelve notebooks in a bag and I took the bus to go to my brother's. Edgar lives in another city. He lives alone in a small apartment. He is finishing his university degree in literature. He is truly, in every way, my big brother. He inherited all the best from our family: our father's charm, our mother's tenacity and clairvoyance, none of their bad habits, their pettiness. I'm in awe of Edgar. Beside him, I feel inferior and awkward, stunted like a plant neglected in his shade. I am a little family hangover he considers beneath even mentioning to his friends. He hadn't even bothered to offer me a copy of his *Midnight Deluge.* He thinks I am too sluggish to understand his poetry. When he sees me in his front doorway, he thinks I'm a madwoman. He finds me repulsive with my enormous eyes and my shaved skull. During my four months of sleepless nights I never thought about the deterioration of my body.

DOCTOR LIMESTONE:
Excellent, excellent.

GABY:
Edgar is angry. He thinks I ran away from home. He pushes me into the bathroom. He shouts that my

smell takes his breath away. I don't waste any time. I unpack my bag.

DOCTOR LIMESTONE:
You tell your brother that you came to read him the most beautiful novel in the world.

GABY:
Yes, Bob.

DOCTOR LIMESTONE:
He doesn't hear you. He grabs the shower hose and tries to turn on the tap. He screams. "What happened to my little sister that she smells so badly?"

GABY:
Yes, Bob. "What happened to my little sister that she smells so badly?"

DOCTOR LIMESTONE:
You open the first notebook. You start to read. From the very first word, Edgar listens.

GABY:
Yes, Bob. Exactly.

DOCTOR LIMESTONE:
You read the twelve notebooks in one stretch. Edgar listens without budging, sitting on the bathtub.

GABY:
Exactly, Bob.

DOCTOR LIMESTONE:
At dawn, when you close up the last notebook, you see a tear on your brother's cheek.

GABY:
A tear, Bob, exactly, a single and unique tear. It slashes me like a knife. Edgar asks me who is the author of the notebooks. But I know he already knows the answer. I tell him: "I am." He answers: "It's still

whistling in my ears. Your sentences snapped my bones. What spirit can possibly stay intact after this flurry? Sister, I am dismembered. Who are you? How many brains live in your shaved skull? Your novel — enormous. An enormous box. But, otherwise, is it truly a novel? It is a galaxy which tramples time. Gaby, you have written the most beautiful novel in the world."

DOCTOR LIMESTONE:

You have won. You have surpassed Balzac.

GABY:

Yes, Bob, I have won. I go to get in the bathtub with Edgar. My head is spinning. I have the impression the bathtub tears itself out of the floor. Edgar and I drift in a space ship, infinitely alone. I don't know how long we are out of this world. It's Edgar who stirs first. He says: "I'm going to make coffee." He gathers up my twelve notebooks and goes to the kitchen. I stay still, glued to the bottom of the bathtub, still floating in the memory of this perfect moment. Suddenly, I am flooded by a premonition. I rush into the kitchen. Edgar is not there. I call him. I look in the other rooms. I shout his name. Edgar has left with my twelve notebooks. For a number of days, I await his return. In vain. I take the bus again. When I glimpse the lights of my city, I release the tears I am holding back. Some months pass. I am dead. I write no more. One day, a letter posted in Africa arrives. I recognized Edgar's writing on the envelope. "I am the happiest of men." His letter starts with this sentence. It's as if I were stabbed by a knife. I had imagined my brother lost, maybe dead or mad. He writes that he is the happiest of men. To live, he need only to open the first notebook and read. People come forward and listen, no matter what language they speak. When he closes the notebook people give him food and drink and don't wait for him to finish eating before asking him to read on. He opens the second notebook, reads it. When he closes it, people would give their very shirts off their backs to hear him read on again. He opens the third notebook, reads it. The people huddle together in the sun and, in a state of grace, lean their heads forward the better to hear. When at dawn, he closes the twelfth notebook, a crowd bows down at his feet ready to give their lives in gratitude. It is thus that my brother gets to discover the gigantic cities, the red skies, the earth damp with dew, the villages hanging on the mountainside. Women driving luxury cars attend to the least of his desires. Politicians scramble to have the honour of serving him. Everyone, from the lowest to the highest, dreams of acquiring his friendship. "My life has become the most beautiful novel in the world." His letter ends with that one sentence. My brother gives no address where I might reply to him. Nor did he even bother to ask news of me. Perhaps he believes that after his escape, I became the happiest of women. He is wrong. I became the unhappiest of women. I tear my brother's letter up. But, in fact, I tear myself up. I love him. I love my brother at the very moment I begin to hate him. I wrote the most beautiful novel in the world for him, for him alone, not for me. I now understand the turmoil that flooded over me in the bath. I was wallowing in the smell of my brother, in the warmth of his skin which my legs brushed against, in the dark bruise of his eyes, in my untamed desire to see the face of the man he had hid from me. How I detest him!

DOCTOR LIMESTONE:
Yes! Yes! Go on! Excellent! Go on!

GABY:
How I detest him! How I detest him!

DOCTOR LIMESTONE:
Don't stop, go on!

GABY:
How I detest him, detest him, detest him/

Knocking is heard at the door.

BALZAC:
It's me! It's me! Open up, it's me!

GABY:
detest him, detest him, detest him/

BALZAC:
Me, Balzac! Open up, Gaby!

GABY:
Balzac!

BALZAC:
Oh what have you done? You deserve to be punished as an example to others.

GABY:
Balzac!

BALZAC:
You know what you are? An infected hag! A slut! A jerk-off! A cum-sucker! A dolly slit! A shit ass! Oh what have you done? Claiming to surpass me, me, Balzac! The most beautiful novel in the world! Don't make me laugh, Gaby! Fly shit, that's all you can produce! Open the door, I'm going to eat you all up, I'm going to dismember you, yank out your eyes, swallow you, make you disappear, digest you and expel you into nothingness. You're just a little shit of a girl, a ridiculous adolescent stuffed with pretension! Surpass Balzac!? Who do you think you are, you little cunt? Open up, I'm going to eat you. Open, Gaby, open up!

GABY:
No! No!

BALZAC:
I'm going to eat you all up!

GABY:
No!

DOCTOR LIMESTONE:
Don't stop, go on!

GABY:
No!

DOCTOR LIMESTONE:
Go on, Gaby, go on!

GABY:
No! I can't anymore, I can't.

DOCTOR LIMESTONE:
Your story isn't finished. Go on!

GABY:
I can't anymore!

She quickly gathers up her clothes, slipping into her dress.

DOCTOR LIMESTONE:
What are you doing?

She heads towards the door.

GABY:
I can't anymore.

DOCTOR LIMESTONE:
You can't leave.

She tries to open the door without success.

I warned you.

GABY:

Open up! Open up!

BALZAC:

Open up, little cunt! I'm going to eat you all up! The most beautiful novel in the world! Yeah, a pack of shit!

DOCTOR LIMESTONE:

You haven't finished your story, Gaby. Finish it. Go right to the end. It is written in the prospectus: one must go right to the end. Go on.

GABY:

I can't!

LENORE:

But what are you doing in your room for the love of God? You're going to drive me mad, Gaby, drive me mad!

DOCTOR LIMESTONE:

Go on! You said you tore up your brother's letter. What did you do after that?

GABY:

My story is over. Finished.

DOCTOR LIMESTONE:

You did something!

DOCTOR MORTIMER:

The last time, it didn't hurt. I don't see why it would this time. Open up. Open wide, wide, wide!

LEA:

I spoke to God. God forgives you. But you need to pray, pray, pray!

DOCTOR LIMESTONE:

What did you do after tearing up your brother's letter? What, Gaby? What?

GABY:

I don't remember anything anymore.

LENORE:

Why are you lying to your mother? Don't you see how I suffer? You are nasty! Nasty!

ALFRED:

You deserve to be punished as an example to others.

LEA:

Mommy doesn't want me to play with you anymore. You are dangerous.

ALFRED:

Gaby, your mother is dead. Open up.

LENORE:

I couldn't bear to live any longer.

ALFRED:

It's your brother's death that killed her.

LENORE:

Who could've, well who could've imagined such horrible suffering? My son, my son, what happened to my son?

LEA:

Is it true what they say? That your brother has been found dead? That's exciting! It seems that his body was atrociously mutilated. Just like in the movies. Is it true, Gaby, that his tongue had disappeared? Is it true, Gaby, that a needle had been driven into the roof of his mouth? A long, very very long needle! Is it true? These are just stories aren't they? Nothing but stories!

GABY:

I feel sick.

Doctor Limestone:

No, no, don't faint, no matter what. Bob is going to finish the story for you.

Gaby:

Don't touch me!

Doctor Limestone:

After having torn up your brother's letter, you opened a notebook, you took the gold-plated Parker and you wrote another story.

Gaby:

Go way!

Doctor Limestone:

Somewhere in Africa/

Gaby:

Shut up!

Doctor Limestone:

Somewhere in Africa lives a woman with the evocative name of Flybelly/

Gaby:

Shut up!

Doctor Limestone:

since her eyes contained the reflections of a Bottle Fly speared by the sun.

Gaby:

Just shut up!

Doctor Limestone:

All the people of the village respect and fear her. This woman is invested with supernatural powers. She heals but also punishes, sickens and kills.

Gaby:

How do you know this story?

DOCTOR LIMESTONE:

One day, a stranger appears at the edge of the village. No one knows where he comes from.

GABY:

Then who are you?

DOCTOR LIMESTONE:

Very quickly, he is encircled by gazes but also by spears and knives. The stranger sets down his backpack, takes out a notebook and reads. The people of the village set down their spears and knives. When he closes the notebook again, silence whistles gently above the palm and banana trees.

GABY:

It's impossible. You are dead, dead!

The rhythms of a tom-tom are heard getting closer.

DOCTOR LIMESTONE:

The next day, the man opens a second notebook before a mob of men but also of women and children. When he finishes the reading, the village drums start on their own to beat a new and intoxicating rhythm. The following day, the man opens a third notebook before a mob of men, women, children but also animals. When he finishes his reading, a scented rain falls from the heavens and in a few seconds makes iridescently beautiful flowers grow. Flybelly witnesses the wonders of the stranger. On the seventh day she is thunderstruck by love when, after having closed the seventh notebook, the man's appearance subtly changes. His white skin darkens throwing off copper reflections in the flicker of the torches. His shirt melts on his shoulders, trickles like hot wax down onto his thighs, and his now naked torso is covered with tattoos inscribing mysterious alphabets on his flesh. His hair puffs up and blossoms like a black water lily which opens under the rays of the moon. His face stretches into an immaculate white smile which is imprinted on Flybelly's heart.

He takes off his shirt revealing his torso covered with tattoos and sacrificial markings.

GABY:
You are dead, a thousand times over. I killed you!

DOCTOR LIMESTONE:
She approaches him. With a single gesture she drops the robe she is wearing and kneels at his feet. In front of the village gathered in full force, she shamelessly offers herself to the man. The man doesn't even look at her and disappears into the forest where, ever since his arrival, hc has gonc to sleep. All the villagers break out in mocking laughter that fills Flybelly's heart with vengeance. Humiliated, one finger in her sex, she looks at the throng and pours forth threats. On the twelfth day, Flybelly cuts the twelve braids from her head and offers them to the God of Night. From earth mixed with her urine, she makes a figurine on which she places twelve drops of the wax she had collected at the feet of the stranger. Then she traces on the ground the same signs she had seen appear on his torso. When the sun half sets behind the horizon, she pours poison into the figurine's mouth. There she implants a long needle. She burns the figurine in the flame of a candle. She slashes it with a knife. Then, she throws stones which break it apart and destroy it.

The mysterious beauty of DOCTOR LIMESTONE's painted torso has attracted GABY. With the tips of her fingers, she traces the designs.

Night arrives. The man opens the twelfth and last notebook in the presence of all the inhabitants of the village but also of the hundreds who have hurried in from the surroundings and of herds of animals which had never before come together without immediately devouring each other. Even the torches that light the centre of the village burn with excitement.

GABY:

As soon as you pronounce the first word of the twelfth and last notebook, a horrible odour escapes from your mouth. Then your tongue swells, writhes and falls off leaving a clear passage for a howl of misery. Sores open on your body liberating pestilent blood which drives the animals insane. An indescribable carnage ensues devastating the village and the forest.

She embraces him.

DOCTOR LIMESTONE:

Flybelly alone, survives. But she has to go very far away into exile for no one dared, since that fatal night, to lay foot in the ruins of her village.

GABY:

I love you.

DOCTOR LIMESTONE:

And I—I hate you. You are going to pay for your crime. It's unacceptable for a girl of sixteen to write a masterpiece. I, Edgar Wrenfield, am the writer in the family. Who won the Eldred-Woodworth Prize for his book of poetry? I did! Who is the most promising poet of his generation? I am! My book *Midnight Deluge* seduced all the critics. You—you just piss rose water. Stick to your cotton print dresses and don't come playing in my sandbox. I hate you, you little cunt. You pretend to suffer from writer's block. All the better to put me to sleep. To make me think that your imagination has dried up, that I don't have to keep an eye on you anymore. A lie. I'm on the lookout, I watch you, I analyze you. I haven't become senile yet, even if in your sickly imagination, you rig me up with such a ridiculous name — Doctor Limestone! You obviously didn't want me to recognize myself. You — feeding me all those pseudo intellectual ideas about underwear! And all those vacuous sentences you made me say about the prospectus, yeah, therapeutic method, my ass. And Balzac! You don't give a damn about Balzac! All you want is to live out your sordid little sexual fantasies. I'm right, aren't I? Look at yourself! You dream up the most grotesque subterfuges just so you can undress in front of me, you give me another skin, black as coal, you amuse yourself by making me suffer, by tearing my flesh, you rub yourself against me, you hug me, you're disgusting, I'm your brother, Gaby, you have no right to gratify your sexual impulses on me, it's incest, it's a crime!

GABY:

What are you afraid of, Edgar?

DOCTOR LIMESTONE:

Afraid! Me!

GABY:

Yes, you! You know what you are? Nothing but a Bob. And you know what a Bob is? A Bob is a prick, a bastard, a man who is afraid for his little prick, for his little talent which is just good enough to ejaculate a tiny poem every six months! You're afraid of me because you can't stand your little sister having more talent, more imagination, more daring than you!

DOCTOR LIMESTONE:

You're going to pay for what you just said.

GABY:

You threaten me! You're ridiculous. You're my creation. You do, you say, exactly what I want you to do and say. You understand, Bob?

DOCTOR LIMESTONE:

That's over. It's all over. You want to play? OK, we'll play. You want to get rid of your writer's block, so then we'll find the therapeutic method best suited to your real problem. Because you are a virgin, aren't you?

He takes off all his clothes. Then, with his hands, he mixes the different colours tattooed on his torso. He also smears his face. Very quickly, he takes on a terrifying and bestial aspect.

Come on, Gaby, plunge. For once, go for it, right to the very end.

Knocking is heard at the door. Immediately we hear the noises of wild animals: lions, tigers, gorillas …

GABY:

You're revolting.

DOCTOR LIMESTONE:

That's what you like. Plunge into evil, Gaby. Plunge into poetry, plunge into blackness. Dare! Dare! Dare!

GABY, drawn, bewitched, advances towards him. Lights fade. The noise of the wild animals increases simultaneously and proportionally as darkness invades the room. Black. Knocking is heard at the door. The animal noises fade out. The light fades up. DOCTOR LIMESTONE is alone. He holds the ventriloquist dummy in his hands.

TALIHUANA:

Parker! Parker! What are you doing holed up in your bedroom? I don't want any more of this!

DOCTOR LIMESTONE:

I'm not doing anything, Mommy.

TALIHUANA:

I heard funny noises. Is someone in there with you?

DOCTOR LIMESTONE:

Why would you think there'd be someone else in my room?

TALIHUANA:

So if you're not doing anything in there and you're alone, why bother to lock yourself in? Parker, I know you're doing something wrong in there, I know, I'm not insane. Open the door, Parker!

DOCTOR LIMESTONE:

Ya, ya, I'm going to open it.

TALIHUANA:

Right away! You're playing with your doll again! Aren't you? You're not a normal boy! At your age, boys don't behave like that anymore. I'm ashamed of you. You're a man, Parker. Men don't lock themselves in their bedrooms and play with dolls. Men go out in the street and work. They build the world. They like women, flesh and blood women, and they make babies, real ones. Are you paying attention to me, Parker?

DOCTOR LIMESTONE:

Yes, Mommy.

TALIHUANA:

You have an appointment soon with Doctor Limestone. Put on clean underwear.

DOCTOR LIMESTONE:

Oh Mom!

TALIHUANA:

It's exactly the sort of thing you forget. I'll be back in five minutes. I want you clean, dressed, combed. Do you hear me, Parker?

DOCTOR LIMESTONE:

Yes, Mommy. (*to the doll*) Hello.

DOLL:
Hello.

DOCTOR LIMESTONE:
Have you got something to tell me?

DOLL:
Yesterday was my birthday.

DOCTOR LIMESTONE:
How old were you?

DOLL:
Twenty-seven.

DOCTOR LIMESTONE:
My, that's good. That's really very good.

DOLL:
It's not all that good.

DOCTOR LIMESTONE:
Twenty-seven—that's wonderful. That's the best age.

DOLL:
I don't know.

DOCTOR LIMESTONE:
I'm sure you must have had a lovely party for your twenty-seventh birthday.

DOLL:
No. Yes. No.

DOCTOR LIMESTONE:
Now, something is bothering you.

CURTAIN.

Translator's Acknowledgements

Much thanks to Christian Bédard for the first translation of the "vulgar, shameful, icky" bits; to Playwrights' Workshop Montreal and Paula Danckert (dramaturge); to Iris Turcott; to the National Arts Centre and Lise Ann Johnson (literary manager); to actors Meg Roe, Nigel Shawn Williams, Bruce Dinsmore, Carmen Grant, Kate Hurman and Kris Joseph; to Le Centre des auteurs dramatiques; and to the Canada Council for the Arts.

Keith Turnbull